# Terminated!

## What Now?

Dorothy Pehowic, LMHC

*Things you wish you knew.*

# Terminated!

## What Now?

Dorothy Pehowic, LMHC

*Things you wish you knew.*

*Note: For the full experience, also purchase the accompanying workbook: "Workbook, Terminated! What NoW?, Things You wish You knew." ISBN: 979-8-9992752-1-9

# Table of Contents

# Preface

Welcome to my book, 'Terminated, What Now? Things You Wish You Knew.' Being terminated, whether you choose to terminate your employment or you were terminated 'out of the blue' and didn't see it coming in a personal dynamic. Ask yourself if you are either physically, financially, mentally, or all of these above stranded and in shock. I hope that with some of the techniques that are focused more on the mental health toll while building a skillset to aid you while you could be facing these circumstances before, during, and after this type of traumatic ordeal. It does not matter if you made $8.00 USD an hour or even $1,000.00 USD an hour. Being terminated, 'pushed-out,' voluntarily, etc., can still leave one feeling alone, abandoned, angry, or even depressed.

You can also apply this book and the accompanying workbook skills to being terminated in a relationship, whether professional or personal. In some cases, we can really not see the ending of your social interactions coming.

My hope for you is that you receive out of this as much as you put into the skills that are Cognitive Behavioral Therapy (CBT) based and are brought forward to aid in your recovering from the set-back that you might feel. Each section is written individually, or you can also apply this book as a whole. This way, if you are looking for a specific skill, you can easily browse the table of contents to find a specific skill or situation that might best suit your situation. It is fully recommended. However, if you apply the entire book and its workbook companion, my hope is that you learn future skills that might aid you in preventing or even preparing for future possible employment or personal relationship downfalls.

Lastly, this book and the accompanying workbook are in no way a replacement for mental, legal or physical health assistance with a licensed provider. IF you begin to identify emotional, safety, legal or mental issues while processing this information, it is strongly recommended to seek out the assistance with a licensed mental, legal or medical provider. This writer is not responsible for any mental or emotional health issues that are unknown by you the reader or this writer and does not assume any liability for providing this skill building platform.

# *Chapter 1*

# What does T*ermination* Mean?

There you are stunned. You have just been notified that you were, 'terminated,' 'Fired,' 'Let go,' 'It's not you, it's me,' 'You just do not fit in here.' 'You're odd,' 'We don't want you here.''It is done, over.' However you have heard it, you have been permanently let go. Your professional or personal relationship has been severed either jointly (agreed on both sides) or by the other person, entity, group of people. whomever. You could feel like you have been marked with a huge letter on your chest with a drumming person following you around town to let everyone in your society know that you have not only been terminated but that there is an expectation that you will now be ostracized   humiliated, bullied, shammed whether is it is on social media.  Or, when you fill out another job application and have to answer honestly if you were voluntarily quitting or that you quit with a termination pending, or just simply terminated. The interesting part is, most do not take into consideration that the workplace, relationship, social network in that area was toxic, unhealthy or even bullied you out. It's just simply accepted that, you are the problem and thus must be made known publicly and personally. Sure, you could choose to never mention the previous employment on your applications and resumes, or even that 'ex,' who lives a block away from other people. However, you will always know that, it didn't work out.

# What does *Termination* Mean?

What exactly does, 'Termination,' mean? ":end in time or existence: CONCLUSION…" (Merriam-Webster,n.d.)

Let's try to break this down a bit. You've hopefully heard the phrase, 'information is power.' Why? Your brain, with no eyeballs or concept of time has no way of knowing at times if an event is happening now or that it happened earlier in life. It is responding simply by the stimuli (senses if you will) that you are feeding your brain. Are you 'hangry'? Then your brain could be interpreting this as, 'Anxiety, we must be in danger let's respond to that the way we always have that has worked best for us.' Thus, if you are hungry but also feel under pressure at any given moment, you might find yourself responding to yourself and others as if your very life is in danger.

Consider this; Depending on your childhood, and how your major caregivers raised you to accept changes in life, and the household directly affects how you personally interpret the ending of relationships. Or, dare I say, 'Healthy Boundaries?' You have to ask yourself if you were ever allowed to say, 'No, thank you.' If you were always told, 'You just have to accept that they are…' Instead of, 'You have permission to say no, and I will keep you safe from them.' Or, 'You are going to let them kiss you, and don't embarrass me if you don't.' Concerning yet, 'You're a fraidie cat.' (bullying)  If you were never given the opportunity to say, 'No,' then this could be playing a role in how you are responding to the ending of a relationship. Lastly, were you ever made fun of for the shaming term, 'Overthinking'? Let's attempt to break this down a bit.

# Chapter 2

# Termination with an Employer

"I just can't do this anymore; it's hard to go to work anymore. I'm terrified every day that I'm making more mistakes because I can't focus anymore."

It is a very common event in today's workforce for an employer, manager, or boss to decide they no longer want you working there. This may happen for various reasons: They do not simply like you as a person, they didn't choose to hire you but someone else did, they see you as a threat to their position, someone else wanted your position and has a connection with your supervisor and now they are both working to 'flush you out,' they can no longer financially afford you to work there, or you blew the whistle too many times on illegal or unethical practices. But are these 'viable' reasons to 'let you go?' Will they 'push' you out by creating a workplace so hostile that it becomes literally impossible to remain working there? You are probably not surprised that they then gaslight you to their lawyers once you leave. However, you still have bills to pay, food that needs to be bought, and possibly other family members who are counting on your earnings, which keeps you going back, trying your best.

You see the hostile attempts, the 'plan' that Human Resources (HR) puts you on to further micromanage you. You are now professionally and socially ostracized. To add insult to injury, your co-workers, in good faith, begin secretly texting or talking to you to show their support out of fear that if they are heard or found to support you, they too might be put on the 'plan.' You are fully aware that they hold you to a different standard than others, and the list of experiences goes on. Or, they just cut to the chase and let you go with no explanation. You can watch copious amounts of videos on the internet from Human Resource (HR) professionals teaching others the various legal verbiage to say the same thing: 'You simply do not fit in.' Everyone wants to be included, to 'fit in.' It is a primal instinct to survive.

As you read the email or letter that has been produced on their behalf, whether it is a full page or a simple sentence, it all says the same thing: You are no longer accepted here. To add to the mass of feelings – sadness, anger, depression, to name a few – they add on the caveat of the 'walk of shame.'

This walk has been seen around the world in countless movies where you are carrying a box with trinkets, papers, and maybe a stapler from the place where you spend one-third of your life. It does not matter if you were only employed for a week, a month, or even fifteen years. Everyone sees it. Everyone knew about it before you, and some had been talking about it, especially in upper management.   As you pack your box, you hold back the tears and the uncomfortable 'goodbye, I'll call you later,' which hardly ever comes.   Then comes the 'settlement.' Are you compelled by the company to sign a 'Do not discuss' letter so that no one else can know their work environment, allowing them to protect themselves legally, socially, or professionally? And if you do not sign it, do they threaten to 'expose' you professionally, adding further injury to what they have already accomplished? Or was it a mutual termination – that you quit, but their response was to terminate you because they were upset that you did not give them the opportunity to terminate you?  Did they do this knowing that in your next job interview, you will possibly look like the 'problem' employee, thus financially abusing you further?

# Termination with an Employer

When it comes to finances, this event could trigger a severe survival mode from death by suddenly not having a steady paycheck, regularity, belonging, and being accepted (i.e., protected as being 'one of the ones'). Again, this is a primal response, and your brain could be operating out of your primal instincts. This could be activating your brain's steam, producing serotonin, and shutting down your fine motor skills to think and react clearly. In this stage, it is strongly recommend to obtain an employment lawyer. They will aid you when paperwork is put before you to sign. It is often suggested to consult an employment attorney when you have the first 'warning,' verbally or in writing, that you are 'on notice.' Some companies, aware of their toxic environment, might actually perform consultations with attorneys around your town so that they become biased, and you might not be able to retain any legal assistance. Once you have had your consultations, you can explore your legal options on how to exit gracefully. If the company is causing harm, committing fraud, wrongful termination, etc., you could be protected by your new legal defense if it comes to that. You might reach an agreement to mutually walk away from this position with a promise that no harm will be done to you. It is always recommended to work directly with a professional Doctor of Law who knows what the laws are, instead of relying on a neighbor, this writer, friend, or family member who has zero legal training.

Let the lawyer think for you so you can focus on self-care. Also, when you are in a calm state when things are actually going well or when you first start at a position, you could write a simple brief 'exit plan.' The purpose of this exit plan is to identify thoughts and impressions that are affecting your workplace, gather resources, and prepare for a safe, quick, and calm exit to protect your mental health as well as future endeavors. You could know within the first week if 'this job' will work out for you. You could know if it is a toxic environment and to the extent that the company will go to protect it. Look for any red flags and do not dismiss them. You could keep this plan updated either monthly or quarterly. Know your emotional, mental, financial, etc., limitations. However, in some workplace environments, you could be blindsided without an exit strategy, left with anxiety and the inability to get out of bed, or have panic attacks in the parking lot when you arrive at work.

# Termination with an Employer

If this is where you are while reading this book, know that you are not alone. Thousands of people around the world day go through this very scenario every day. Below are some Wikipedia statistics from 2024 in the United States National statistics for workplace bullying. The stats are astounding:

'…from the 2007 WBI-Zogby survey show that 13% of U.S. employees report being bullied currently, 24% say that they have been bullied in the past, and an additional 12% say they have witnessed workplace bullying. Nearly half of all American workers (49%) report that they have been affected by workplace bullying, either being a target themselves or having witnessed abusive behavior against a co-worker.' (Wikipedia contributors, 2024)

Additionally,

'… The scientific study determined that almost 75% of employees who were surveyed had been affected by workplace bullying, whether as a target or a witness.' (Wikipedia contributors, 2024)

However, with that said, it still doesn't take away the sting of these statistics. Let's work together through these pages on how to re-frame your new experience in this venue. If you find that you need to process this traumatic experience, I recommend consulting a licensed professional counselor who specializes in trauma to give you further coping skills as well as the ability to spot this type of professional social behavior prior to applying to your next position.

Let's review a possible termination from a more personal standpoint.

# *Chapter 3*

# **Personal Relationship**

"I keep getting told out of the blue that I need to change to make them or their family happy. If I don't, then I'm made fun of or even threatened by other people who know them."

You can see this type of dynamic as early as in childhood. Were you ever bullied (continuously made fun of or told over and over again the demands of another person regardless of how it made you feel)? You just gave in and involuntarily performed the tasks that were demanded of you. Once you did that, you were reminded over and over, 'You did it that one time, so I know you can do it.'

Or, you feel that you have no options. This is seen a lot of the times with children; they literally do not have any options other than to allow a major caregiver to impose their will. At times, you might see different responses such as, 'friending,' where they try their best to gain the approval of that major caregiver to avoid further punishment - i.e., being made fun of – to be accepted so someone else will receive the mental/verbal/physical shaming or punishments. This can be seen as becoming the 'recruited' by the abusive person to where they now perform the same shaming and punishments to another family member to gain the approval or acceptance of that abusive person.

Or, in a dating scenario. The 'controlling partner' has ostracized you from your family (i.e., recruited your parents with kindness so that they accept them more than you and force you to stay with them. Or, their very own family perform this task knowing that you will not tell your family or former friends because you know that they will not support you.) and yet, they seek out personal affirmations from other people around and in front of you, thus adding to the shaming that you feel at every event.

Lastly, siblings or extended family such as cousins, etc., who make fun of you (bully you) make it clear that they will be friends on social media but will not go out of their way to maintain any type of relationship with you unless it is solely to benefit them.

With each event, you feel the ending of that relationship coming near. You might even secretly wish for some catastrophic event that would separate you from them so you wouldn't have to terminate the relationship and look like 'the bad guy'. The whole time throughout your life, all you hear is, 'You do not belong here,' followed by being abandoned, ostracized emotionally or even physically, with a dash of humiliation.

What about your support system? This could include friends or your social network.

# *Chapter 4*

# **Social Support System**

You throw a housewarming party for your new home, but no one shows up. You follow up with your 'people,' and they all have reasons for not being there or even telling you in advance that they wouldn't attend. Your heart sinks into rejection because you told them about the housewarming for months. Every time you run into an acquaintance in the group, you always hear, 'We need to get together for coffee sometime,' but it never happens. You go to your place of worship/social group and find that your things are moved from your seat and that spot is surrendered to another person without your consent. You always have to make the effort to be included in their events after hearing about them through the 'grapevine,' but your invitation always seems to get lost. You are quoted a phrase with an expectation of humility or something that justifies their boundary crossing with you so that they continue to feel justified in doing this to you repeatedly. Lastly, you are declined when you make attempts to volunteer because you are single, 'married to the 'wrong person,' or you just do not seem to 'fit in.'

# Social Support System

How many of you have felt terminated, abandoned in plain sight, and disconnected like the above? It happens more often than not. (Keep in mind, these are just examples.) If you notice a person who was attending your 'socials' and then suddenly stopped, chances are they might not feel like they belong. Sometimes, a predominant person in the group is challenged or does not like you, the rest follow suit to 'avoid confrontation.' Or, they fear that they might be treated like you and become terminated from the group. However, in many cases, they received that message from someone or many someones in the group or gathering.

When a person experiences these personal events, they can really dig deep into any insecurities or fears that they might have already had from childhood. Some handle it differently; they become more social or volunteer more to the point where they are spending more time volunteering at network social events than at home or with their family. So, their relationships at home are now being affected by this behavior.

# Chapter 5.

# Moving Forward

Moving forward.  Moving forward is the point in most movies where you see the main character being beating, down forgotten, plunged laying helplessly on the ground with no one to support them back up. Then, you hear the music slowly increase in tempo as the camera pans towards the legs of the main character slowly and with purpose suddenly move and take their first step forward. With each step, you hear the drums hit loudly and suddenly all the while the music picks up it's tempo and pitch. The once down and abandoned character is now moving forward to complete the movie. Have you ever noticed that most movies that have a scene like this hardly end with the main character actually giving up? While they are saying, 'well, we did the best that we could,'? No way! If it did, What or who would you cheer for? How hopeless would you feel after the feelings of investment that grew in you about this character as you were becoming absorbed in the movie?  In this case, YOU are the main character.

No one, not even this author can tell you how to move forward, you choose. At this point in the book and it's accompanying workbook, you have been given skills on how to identify your choices that have led you to where you are today. You also learned, what was in and outside of your control and how to regain your control of your life, purpose and future. At the end of the day, moving forward is one of the hardest decisions that one will have to make. It is your choice, time and effort that chooses not only when but how you will choose to move forward. Will it be scary? It depends on how you are with adaptation and change. Do you feel that you need additional support emotionally, physically, or mentally with moving forward? In the previous chapters there have been several suggestions on how to do this. In the reference portion, you will also find additional supporting agencies who can help you mentally. But, at the end of the day, it will come completely up to you.  The key point, 'when you are ready.'  This is in YOUR TIME. I can not convey this enough. This is your narrative no one else. Your success will be based on your choices and effort, no one else's. Below is one last skill that I created called, 'Calendaring.' - Dorothy Pehowic, 2020.

While working with a client through their overwhelming anxiety with life  I found myself creating this tool that has become a staple in many of my sessions with clients:

# *Chapter 6*

# **Resources**

Resources are always good to compile throughout life. You never know when you might need a referral or resource. Below are a few resources that have already been mentioned in this book for various purposes. I have also included a few that have not been.

988, The United States national Crisis and Suicide Hotline.

800-273-8255, National Suicide Prevention Hotline.

National Institute of Mental Health (NIMH): https://www.nimh.nih.gov/health/find-help.

In this website, you will find links and phone number for immediate assistance. This also includes for military veterans.

National Alliance on Mental Illness (NAMI): https://www.nami.org. (800) 950-6264. Text: 62640 text: 'helpline'.

# Resources

At this website, you will find the national Alliance on Mental Illness where they maintain consistent train with peer staff members who volunteer their time to always be accessible for any assistance that you might need. They also include information for recovery support, depression and eBooks as well as seminars for family and friends for additional support.

Psychology Today. www.psychologytoday.com.

This website is derived from the United States National network of, American Counseling Association. This is the National governing body for, Licensed Professional Counselors. Psychology Today is a website where many of the licensed and registered clinicians around the United States have been professionally vetted and verified if they are licensed, interning, life coach, etc. It will also help you to understand the differences of the various licenses and requirements to receive this level of training.

Substance Abuse and Mental Health Services Administration (SAMHSA): https://www.samhsa.gov/.

This website include mental health assistance not only for substance abuse but mental health in general to include disaster distress and the national helpline.

The Vet Center: https://www.vetcenter.va.gov/. (877) 927-8387.

This website is for any current or previous military service member to call or visit for mental health counseling. This facility is a clinic outside of the Veterans Administration Hospital's and clinics. They provide licensed mental health clinicians outside of the VA system working with either combat service or military sexual trauma (MST). Free of charge. There is a Vet Center located outside of most major cities and near each VA regional system.

# Resources

Veterans Administration (VA): https://mental health.va.gov/. (800) 698-2411.

This is a website for any current or previous military member and their support to call or visit for additional resources. They also include their direct crisis hotline.

# Conclusion

As you reach the end of this journey, it's essential to reflect on the transformative insights you've uncovered. Throughout this book, and the accompanying workbook, you have explored the strategies and mindsets necessary to overcome this challenge, harness personal strengths and you personal identity with healthy boundaries.

**Understanding the situation**: You first learned to identify factually the circumstances that you are currently or will be or have been in. Information is power, you learned by understanding the actual situation and separating the emotions that are surfacing in the situation, how to respond rationally to deplete any possibility of farthing additional harm to yourself emotionally, and hopefully mentally.

**Realizing your ascertainable options and future planning:** Next, you discovered the power of identifying what is reasonable in the immediate and then future planning. You learned how to begin to achieve goals and create actionable plans.

**Building Resilience by establishing Healthy Boundaries:** You explored techniques to build resilience and manage stress as well as life obstacles that are self and other person producing.

**Positive Mindset:** You discovered a reframing way of thinking from 'the old usual ways,' that have quite literally shaped your reality that you have been responding to. By adapting your mindset to a positive one, you will now following through with your actions that will not only affect you but also those around you.

# Conclusion

**Moving Forward:** Lastly, you were given another skill on how to recognize further healthy and unhealthy habits of others and possibly yourself to steer clear of for future success. Now is the time to put these insights into action. Knowledge is only as valuable as its application. Here are some additional steps to get you started:

**Start Small:** Begin with one or two strategies that resonate most with you. Gradual changes often lead to lasting habits. Start with something that is reasonable for you, I.E., Self Care, writing a morning note, Positive Affirmations. Keep it small and simple that you know you can accomplish. This will become rewarded in your brain and build self-confidence the more you apply this skill. You can build on it later.

**Stay Consistent:** Consistency is key, Keep at it even when progress seems slow. Once you rebuild a new habit in the previous time, space, location; your brain might become 'unstuck,' from that preparation. An example: Finding yourself like a broken record recounting to another person the same issues at work, relationship, event to where that is all that you talk about. This keeps your brain with no eyeballs in the same time and place and not moving forward. Instead, be consistent with choosing something different to talk about, or do with other people that does not come close to discussing the previous issues. IF those issues 'need,' to be discussed, it is highly recommended to seek out professional mental health assistance so that you are not affecting your relationships and future career or personal goals by keeping you and those around you in your past and not being present with them. By being consistent with a 'new pattern of behavior,' you will eventually be able to move forward from this situation successfully.

**Reflect and Adjust:** Regularly reflect on your progress and be willing to adjust your approach as needed. An example: 'I did everything right every time but I keep getting treated this way!' Go back to the begging, did you choose the right people, circle of support or career/job for you? Did you originally ignore the red flags of that employer, person, or group of people and therefore choose to

# Conclusion

modify a core belief or a hard boundary of who you are? Then in that aspect, you didn't do 'everything right..' by you. When you choose to be the, 'people pleaser,' you are essentially creating chaos for you and those around you. When you establish healthy boundaries for you (This means not only stating them but also enforcing them as well.), then you are giving permission for you to be perfectly you and them to be perfectly them. When others do not know where your boundaries are because you re not setting them, you could be resenting them instead of being present while they are becoming frustrated with you and not understanding how to be present with you. This can create a hostile and toxic dynamic. 'But I don't want to be alone.' If you are being true to who you are and find those who resinate with you, you won't be. By being authentically who you are, you are giving others and yourself the opportunity to decide if this is your space or not. This way they do not feel manipulated and you can then focus on the job or relationship at hand instead of walking on eggshells and responding impulsively. Lastly, become 'ok,' with being 'different.' You were not created by a cookie cutter. The more you are self accepting, the less you will be tolerant of anything or anyone who could wish you harm for their own
gratification.

Remember, every great journey begins with a single step. Sometimes we're thrown into a change other times we choose them. As you begin your efforts that bring you closer to your envisioned lifestyle celebrate every mile stone. Embrace the process, and learn from your setbacks. You choose your potential and your future.

Thank you for allowing this book to be a part of your journey. Here's to your continued growth and success!

# About the Author

**Dorothy Pehowic:** A Licensed Mental Health Counselor (LMHC), motivational speaker and self-help author writes from a lifetime of service. Dorothy is known for her empathy as she works with those who are in their most vulnerable and to connect them with their own courage. In the book and accompanying workbook, 'Terminated, What Now? Things You Wish You Knew.' Dorothy explores, with the basis of Cognitive Behavioral Therapy (CBT) how to connect the reader to address the least mentioned part of being terminated, their mental health through this process. As the reader ventures through this book they will be able to identify: When to ask for help, what kind of help and how to help themselves for future life experiences while remaining present in their current circumstances. Throughout this process, the reader will identify successful strategies that will aid in their personal future development.

# *REFERENCE*

Merriam-Webster. (n.d.). Boundary. In Merriam-Webster.com dictionary. Retrieved May 16, 2024, from https://www.merriam-webster.com/dictionary/boundary.

Merriam-Webster. (n.d.). Termination. In Merriam-Webster.com dictionary. Retrieved May 16, 2024, from https://www.merriam-webster.com/dictionary/termination.

Wikipedia contributors. (2024, April 13). Workplace bullying. In *Wikipedia, The Free Encyclopedia*. Retrieved 18:28, May 17, 2024, from https://en.wikipedia.org/w/index.php?title=Workplace_bullying&oldid=1218794456.

www.ingramcontent.com/pod-product-compliance
Lightning Source LLC
Chambersburg PA
CBHW060527280326
41933CB00014B/3107